JU MB LED

Seeking the light

a poetry book by
Thsetezela

BLUEROSE PUBLISHERS
India | U.K.

Copyright © Thsetezela 2024

All rights reserved by author. No part of this publication may be reproduced, stored in a retrieval system or transmitted in any form or by any means, electronic, mechanical, photocopying, recording or otherwise, without the prior permission of the author. Although every precaution has been taken to verify the accuracy of the information contained herein, the publisher assumes no responsibility for any errors or omissions. No liability is assumed for damages that may result from the use of information contained within.

BlueRose Publishers takes no responsibility for any damages, losses, or liabilities that may arise from the use or misuse of the information, products, or services provided in this publication.

For permissions requests or inquiries regarding this publication, please contact:

BLUEROSE PUBLISHERS
www.BlueRoseONE.com
info@bluerosepublishers.com
+91 8882 898 898
+4407342408967

ISBN: 978-93-5989-853-7

Cover Design: Muskan Sachdeva
Typesetting: Pooja Sharma

First Edition: March 2024

This book is dedicated to all the wonderful individuals who have crossed my path. And to those who can relate to the experiences shared within the pages

Contents

SOFTLY WILD *1*

PAWS *3*

SHE *6*

SWEET YOUTH *8*

UNHEARD VOICES *9*

MOON *10*

BETRAYAL *12*

SUMMER NIGHTS *14*

SHOULD'VE KNOWN BETTER *16*

SEASON *19*

HER DREAMS *21*

HIS TAG *23*

ESCAPE *25*

DEDICATED *27*

THE FIRST PAIN *28*

HOUDINI *31*

MORNING BLISS *33*

MIRROR *35*

OUT OF THE HOLE *37*

NIGHT BREEZE *39*

STRETCH THE TRUTH *42*

REALITY *45*

WISHES	*46*
GUILT OF LETTING GO	*48*
WORDS CUT	*51*
VALOUR	*52*
ROSE	*53*
THE OTHER ME	*56*
DRESS IN BLUE	*58*
FLAME	*60*
GAS LIGHTING	*61*
JUMBLED	*63*
VISION	*65*
CLARITY	*66*

SOFTLY WILD

She dared to dream,
With her eyes wide open;
With each sunset,
Her dreams were illuminated like the stars
In the night sky.

Though she was asked,
"If she has no fear of the unknown?"
To this, she replied,
"My home was a venom",

This fragile soul of hers,
Has matured within the four walls.
Oblivion of the fact that,
It was fed with the rigid and conventional norms.

She now feel the rot in her soul,
The stench of what she accumulated within;
This venom of old conventional beliefs,
That runs through the bloodline.

When they call her an adventurer,
She put on a subtle smile,
While her entire soul erupts in agony.
For she humbly concedes,
With the truth that she is indeed an adventurer,
In search of love,
For she has received,
The most toxic form of love,
From what she perceived as kin.

Yet she dares to dream with audacity,
For she has foreseen herself,
Bloom with authenticity.
For she dared to break,
The long-rotted generational curse.

She was labelled as a rebel,
But the irony here is,
She envisioned herself as a queen,
Who dared to usurp every barrier,
With the grace of a feminine.

For she knew that within her lay a spark,
That would ignite the world and leave a lasting mark.

PAWS

Soft chips of
God's tiny creation;
A whistle for the
Day to begin.

Cool breeze swiftly
Brushes my skin,
As I sip my
Cup of tea.

With yet another
Three of God's
Lovable creation;
My fur babies.

Adorable and clever,
Pampered and coddled;
Dainty yet defensive;
For their beloved.

From belly rubs
And naps,
To crawling and
Curling for slumber.

What a sight of joy
You are for those
Eyes that catch
A glimpse of you.

From your tiny paws
To now matching
To the size
Of our palm;

A bond connected,
A sprinkle of magic;
With every stroll
You take.

Our black trousers
Are where you
Leave behind most
Of your love.

Strand by strand,
We collect,
And blow it
In the air.

Yet, it still finds
It's way back to us,
Much like your
Eternal Love.

SHE

'Never let go', she whispered to herself,
A swift flare enlightened her dimmed spirit.
Once again she rose up and;
Puffed her deepest secrets,
Up in the breeze.

She knew she was,
An oyster of secrets,
In an ocean full of prey.
Into her fragile arms,
She held on tight to her secrets,
And carried it around like her antique.

Onto the journey of soul search,
A brittle path she is in.
Gently tiptoeing her steps,
Yet she left an ineradicable trace.
When her spark starts to waver,
She takes a sip from,
Her bottle of secrets.

How soothing she felt!
The nothingness within her,
Began to be elevated,
With a swift zeal;
And with it arose ,
Her fiercest passion.

She is on her journey of soul search.
An empress in the making.

SWEET YOUTH

Pink ribbons and ripped jeans,
Neon lights and starry scenes,
The smell of youth and rebel taste,
Oh, those days were such a haste.

Tell me, universe, what I should trade,
To get back that spark that once stayed?
Raindrops remind me of nostalgia,
The slow slide on the window.

Oh, how times have changed so fast,
Now teardrops slide down my cheeks at last,
It's a nightmare, to lose that spark.

UNHEARD VOICES

Stoic thoughts and expressions,
Emotions crumbled in a corner, like a written piece of paper
Waiting to be unfolded, yet so vulnerable to be read.
Crystal clear seemed like an illusion if perfection is an art.
Dilemma and obsession dragged me into this abyss.
If pain were to strike, I would smell its rage from afar.
I prepare my heart for a cold-blooded war.
Who would care? I visualize no one.
Would they even know? I almost bled to death from this wound of sorrow.

Command the wind to whisper into your ear the pain I sighed.
After I had to forgive, to shed all the betrayals that have sunken deep into my soul.

MOON

In the stillness of the night,
The moon shone so bright,
A floating butterfly in the sky,
And the star beside it, a firefly.

Lost in the vastness of the sky,
They seemed separate from the rest,
A true lonely pair, but why?
This empty space, their nest.

As I sat and stared,
They exuded a hesitant grace,
Their calm aura they shared,
Their distance remaining in place.

My heart cheered for them silently,
That night, they shone the brightest,
The night went by ,but memories remain,
Of what could have been, a love in vain.

For they never grew apart, that's true,
Despite the vast sky,
But they never seemed to come closer,
And I believe that what it means Near but not together, forever.

BETRAYAL

I have loved more,
And received a twofold betrayal.
Miserable yet so in love
The oxymoron of life.

A devotee of disillusionment,
For the sake of an ounce of love
Kept pouring until I was mindless
I hated my idiocy.

But love overshadowed and
Ignorance crept in
Fed me with all the lies
Now I despise being genuine.

In my oblivious state of mind
I run back to the lies
That once made me feel loved .
Love is my fiercest armour

I am a fighter,
But I chose the wrong battle
Now my wounds are in vain
And my scars are a reminder

Of my absurdity.
Until my vision gets blurry
And my breath starts to decelerate
I will remember this betrayal

It will be an oath,
Given by the person I once loved.

SUMMER NIGHTS

Sunrays are now laid to rest.
These summer nights have enchanted
the sweetest of aesthete,
to adore this beauty
for yet another page to be filled
with the ink of their deepest secrets.

On one of these summer nights,
a thought struck:
"Why did my dreams feel like a famine?
I thirst for passion,

but the fear in my closet peaks at me.
Ocean of words still lingers,
a prickle in my throat."

There is always a tussle,
do my broken dreams get to live again?
Or it is another whispered goodbye.
On a mellow summer evening,
as the fading sun ray glanced at my doorstep,
I realised that every sunset
is a reminder of how beautiful
the next sunrise would be.

I concede on these summer nights,
the misty moon,
the summer rain,
washed away the guilt
of my broken dreams.
Waves of passion took me away!
The everlasting optimism resurfaces.

Oh! How I adore these summer nights.

SHOULD'VE KNOWN BETTER

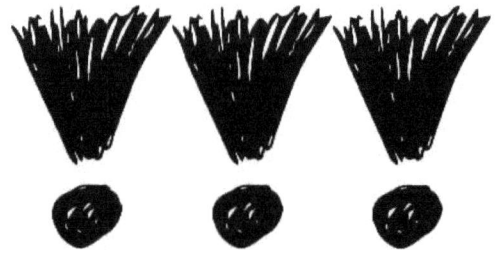

I should have known better,
Better than the rest,
Because each time;
The universe offered me,

a blank slate,
To rewrite my life,
I would rewrite ;
Your name first.

Love became an;
Intricate puzzle,
As I thirst,
For simplicity.

I fooled myself into,
This illusion that,
Flogging a dead horse,
Was what it meant to be loyal.

Our together forever,
Now felt like,
A one-minute tragedy.
A minute of bliss and then fallacy.

The mind always seeking;
for an escape.
Hoping for a paradise,
But realities are to be faced,
And paradise does not exist in a world of lust.

Realizing how abate I was,
This truth suffocated me,
Unheard voices speak to myself;
Taken aback by the reality,

But truth be told,
How naive I was!
Lost in my void,
Lest did I fail to realise;

Everything else was crumbling,
Unable to uphold my mind,
I stand beside my abyss;
With my grand to never fall again.

SEASON

This time of the year,
Waiting for the unfolding
Of a new season,
A spark that gleams,
The eyes along with the heart,
An inkling of unrevealed happiness.

Autumn of concealed joy,
More noise, more crowds,
The smokes go higher,
Streets get busier.

In the midst of it all,
Under the beaming love
Of a thousand stars,
There is a silent spectator
That has seen it all.

A lone soul that
Has walked down the beaten path,
And in the darkness of leisure time,
Has watched The Last leaf
Of the season fall.

The world stopped,
And hope seems like
The two polar poles.

The midnight breeze
Became its soothing music,
Amidst the chaos and calm.

One thing remains forever true,
The changing of the season, old and new.

This change of season
Brings a hope for a renewed spirit,
A winter of joy

HER DREAMS

In the stillness of the night,
She grew and bloomed with grace ,
Lit her lamp of dreams;
A fluorescence of hope.
Her eyelids are a gateway
To the unknown, a new;
Her dreams, a mirror
In her reality,
A source of joy, only in totality.

But some dreams crept fears in her,
Such a dream she had one night;
A lonely bridge she must cross,
Calm waters beside her,
Once loved ones are ahead,
Behind her people who love her.

But the fear of leaving all took flight;
At midnight she stirred and awakened from her dreams.
But she now knows
The path she has to forge;
With the sunrise, she'll take the first step,

For her heart knows the journey ahead.
For her dream a foresight,
Towards her destiny,
And determined to make it a reality.

HIS TAG

He and I loved him like a river,
Love flows and it flowed,
But only towards him.

He tagged me as,
Naive and paranoid.
The irony here is,

I am withered and parched,
For a drop of his love.
I scrutinized my love;

For his apathy.
My eyes have captured him,
As my chevalier.

Ignorant to see the truth,
But the truth is,
He had an ocean of love,
To be poured.
Sigh! he was pouring it,
On another beauty.

Down the line,
I still have his tag on,
As a souvenir.

ESCAPE

If ever there's a space
Unseen with the naked eye,
Do you yearn to make it your own,
A place of solace, so unknown?

I would hasten myself away
From half-empty crowds,
To make that space
As my shelter.

I would dethrone every possible title
To call it
The only home that
I have ever known.

Like every escapist,
There is always a muse,
An abstract that would
Make them the utopian dreamer.

Beneath the twinkling stars, I lay.
I lose myself;
Ignorance and ecstasy
Are intertwined so well.

I knew that this is
My ticket to paradise.

DEDICATED

Sometimes a person can
Remind you of how lost you are.
To you my emancipator,
You are the irony.

A soul that usurped all my bitterness,
With you, I have reached my zenith.
In you, I have found my solace.
You, my knight, made me realize that
Life is never meant to walk on a tightrope.

How swiftly you made me realize
How easy it is to let it all go.
What a blunder has my life been,
And this is how I realized how lost I was before I met you.

The stars are now smitten
By the love that shines so bright in you.

THE FIRST PAIN

If life has ever gifted you,
Your first ever pain,
What could it possibly be?

I felt the first pain,
When I lost myself,
In a swirl of opinions;

When I lost my sharpness,
To the bluntness,
Of clouded judgments.

I felt the first pain,
When my mind became,
A home for twisted thoughts.

A void so vast,
That I failed to;
Crawl myself out.

I felt the first pain,
When my attempts towards,
My dreams were futile.

And my re attempts were,
Just whispered thoughts.
When I took refuge ;

To inaction while life seemed like,
An oath to be helpless.
To always be guilty as an excuse.

A swift surprise gifted,
To relish in the;
Rough edges of life.

Now, I walk in my grace,
As non of these;
Could ever disdain my soul.

HOUDINI

Adulthood taught me escapism,
To enter a void in which
We played like children
On a merry-go-round.
So contented in this,
We build a home,
Never daring to leave.

We disappeared and got lost in it.
It was a trick that I
Forced myself to learn and
Now it is a part of me,
Like a Houdini for life.

Stuck between the
Two phases of life,
There is a shadow,
A ghost that lingers
From a phase that I
Just freed myself from.

I stand on a stage
Where the old tricks
That I learned
Does not appease the crowd.

I wrap myself in
A thin black cloth
And vanish to
Sink into my solitude.

Time and again,
I have played this act,
To be lost and
Then to disappear,
Lost from the present
And disappear into the
Wilderness of the mind.

Escapism is unsatisfactory,
And the applause no longer
Seems genuine.
In the next stage I am on,
I want to be a performer,
Someone who doesn't just
Disappear,
Someone who's never gone.

MORNING BLISS

Whistles of sweet nature,
Trees sway so gently with the wind,
The world is hushed,
The air is still.

Dew drops clear as crystal,
All around the earth in tranquil,
Chirps as soothing music,
Roosters as Nature's alarm.

The gift of nature,
So raw and pure,
To revitalize as the day begins,
A subtle change in the sky.

A palette of colours,
From shades of red to blue,
Fresh and untouched,
As the world remains unawaken.

The world in deep slumber,
At the brink of their dream,
The joy to witness,
The first Sunray.

The quiet dawn,
Before the sun's first kiss.

Empty roads,
Long and stretched,
Still healing from yesterday's jam.
The silence is defeaning,yet so serene
A chance to breathe,to slow down.
A gift bestowed upon
By nature in the morning bliss
Every day, a masterpiece to view.

MIRROR

In front of the mirror I stand,
My perception often wavers.
Beauty seems like a fleeting dream,
And perception, a reflection of my senses.

Obscured image in front of me,
I am aware that it is me I see.
But have I lost my essence, my core depth?
Am I a mere reflection of past hurts?

The mirror on the wall, I ask,
Am I wailing over memories that passed?
Of past insecurities, remarks that wounded,
And disillusioned judgments that left me haunted.
I despise this reflection of reality.

Am I a mere reflection of what was imposed on me,
Or can I break free and let my true self be?
The inner child that was once wounded,
Now concealed in a jar of secrets unspoken.

A secret that gleams so bright,
Inviting me to heal and make things right.
As I inquest myself, if I ever open the jar,
Will I be able to heal or just dim the light afar?

OUT OF THE HOLE

Dim your light, if you wish to blend in,
Be one among us, don't let your spark win.
For the scent of hypocrisy fills the air,
And the fear of being outshone is everywhere.

In this loop of double standards, hold on tight,
Keep your dreams alive, your mind alight.
Don't let it be a puppet in someone's hand,
Who takes pleasure in controlling life's strand.

Build a fence of perseverance, let it surround,
Your vision, your goals, within its bound.
So that no one absurd enough may dare,
To open their Pandora's box of misery, and impair.

Let discernment be your guiding light,
To segregate between concern and control's sight.
Let no ego be diluted with pleasure,
As soon as they see your sanity's measure.

Let them question your depth of despair,
For they will carry a lifetime of burden to bear.
To even have the audacity to question,
Your strength to emerge out of this pit of abyss.

NIGHT BREEZE

Some nights seem to be
Longer than usual;
Dozing and scrolling,
Pages flipped, coffee spilled.
An uneasy feeling seems to linger.

A soft tease by the breeze
Serves as a gentle reminder
To liberate temporarily.
The cool breeze takes me
Away to a place I have never stepped on;
That place calls for me, and I long for it.

The breeze has taught me
To let go and be light as a thread,
Though the heaviness of being connected
To the worldliness weighs you down.

To be calm in the midst of darkness.

As the breeze swiftly goes by the night,
I whisper my desires and wishes
For the breeze to teach us to be an adventurer like itself,
To be a passer-by who soothes the raging mind
Of those whose heads are heavy with thoughts.

Teach us to be as you, to mimic your softness,
After a long rough day, teach us the art of
Letting our thoughts out with a sigh,
As we lay out sight in the sky,
And you gently pass by.

Some nights we long for you,
As you venture on and in your absence,
Teach us to imitate your peace,
Teach us to be in oneness with nature.

Teach us to seamlessly pass the hurdles of the night,
To see the dawn of a new day.
Oh gentle breeze, how you make us feel
So light and free, how you make us heal
From the worries that weigh us down
And the thoughts that make us frown.

Of a world full of grace,
And a life that's worth the chase.

STRETCH THE TRUTH

Young and supple,
Mind delusion,
A mirage of genuine love
Enticed my undiluted emotions.

My eyes would sparkle
At the sight of this,
I'd reach out my hands
Only to be left feeling alone.

It was too far,
Always too far for me
To unravel their intentions,
But close enough to be able to unmask them.

A temptation for my raging long
To be appreciated,
Pick and choose
The parts and pieces of me,
But never as a whole.

Love and expectations
Weighed at equilibrium,
But if I ever had to
Shatter their expectations,
A kilo of their love
Would be reduced.

Love in the facade
Of expectations,
And here I am again
An alien to love.

Their love felt like the stars,
Always distant, yet appealing,
And when I yearn for their love,
They would send me fireflies
In the form of love, a sweet deception.

The cracks in me thirst for love,
A drop of it would ease my soul.
Passed an entire decade
Of a season of drought
Just left me to death.

Expectations turned into a shield
Of delusion opinions,
A blockage in my path
Was fed with expectations
While left to be hungry for love.

I despised this,
A bitter taste in my mouth,
A taste of coaxed love.
Now I feed myself
With drops of rebellions wrath.

Being a rebel feeds my hunger,
My naive soul
Will never be fooled
Nor starved again.

REALITY

I wish I never believed in FAIRYTALES..
Now I struggle with reality.
No magic spell can cast away the demons,
Except with my WIT.

No magic wand can do wonders,
Except with my own STRENGTH.
No fairies can take me to a faraway land,
Except my DREAMS.

There is never a happy ending,
Just a happy mind in the END.

WISHES

Guilt weighs,
More than a million masses.
A weight that can't be
measured by scales or glasses.

Ever wondered where does
that weight comes from?
A galaxy of unspoken
emotions laid to rest.

They say if you
witness a shooting star,
make a wish and it will go far.
But ever wondered what happens
when it hits?

When it explodes into tiny particles,
those wishes no longer
carries your emotions.
It is now turned into pieces of particles
high above the head
and down below the heaven.

Now the galaxy carries
all your wishes,
those whispered wishes.
And that is the amount of weight a guilt weighs,
a burden so heavy, hard to see the haze.

GUILT OF LETTING GO

Tarnished visions of forever,
Sombre colours,
Withered leaves.
A sight that I now dread,
When waves of memories,
Sway me away from the reality.

Raw and untamed,
We believed in the diamond in the rough,
And yet sigh at the sight of fallen petals.
Swiftly we have, lost this essence.
How oblivion of the illusions we were!

Blindfolded by sombre,
Life felt intoxicated,
Blurry sight and staggering walk,
Reality seemed to be more serene than,
The thoughts that is painted,
Grey inside this mind.

A loud knock of reality stroked,
Emotions now diluted,
With the fear of unknown.
Reality, we despised it.
Yet with a sulky pace,
We are now trapped,
In this maze of harsh reality.

Decisions!
Decisions!

In solitude I lay,
With an empty soul,
Yet the guilt of letting go,
Weighs a million masses.

If I ever had to look back,
I would take another chance to be stabbed.
I'd trade my strides,
For the glimpse of joy,
We lost in the face of reality.

WORDS CUT

Words, oh words, so powerful and true,
Can cut so deep,
Leaving Emotional scars anew,
Not visible to the eye.

Words that strike at you,
With a facade Of Love,
Oh so sharp, the edges now bruised.
Tears became a catalyst,
For the vision to be more clear.

In a vast void,
All alone I created a library of words,
That was once used to tear me down.
Each word I collect, is a treasure to behold.

A beautiful poem, a story yet untold,
For every wound, a word of healing I find.
Words oh words, you have now become,
My beacon of light.

VALOUR

When tears of a lost dream
Keep on rolling,
And your soul could feel the tussle
Between your barren vision
And a void dream.

Let your valour sink it,
Rekindle with yourself once again.
Rekindle your vision
That will soothe your raging desires.

Though a thousand thoughts
May keep you spiralling down
Into an abyss,
Let not your fear of being delusional
Strike your zeal.

ROSE

I held a rose today,
A young bloom!
But it left me
With no choice but to,
Sympathize on all,
The turmoil that,
It has yet to endure.

I see roses blossoming,
As I gaze among the bushes,
Some are carefully nurtured,
In someone's backyard,
Some are wrapped in plastic and,
Others are mismatched in bundles.

We may have shed,
A tear of joy for;
They reminded us
Of the beauty of love.

While it may be a,
A beautiful reminder to some,
Of their long-lost love.

This thread of connectivity,
Between the love of beauty,
And the pain that comes with it.

The depth of being loved,
To be preserved,
Between the pages of,
One's favourite book.

And to be treasured even,
After its death,
A symbol of love that never fades.
A rose.

THE OTHER ME

Stuttering with words,
a path of life wrought,
a journey of pauses and starts,
a flow that's never quite caught.

Sometimes I struggle to let go,
certain words linger, they move too slow,
a battle within a constant fight,
every sound and syllable, a mountain insurmountable in sight.

Whispers of mockery I hear,
behind me, beside me, even from familiar faces, I fear,
to hide my insecurities I put on a show,
so often I lose my voice, and so I turn to my pen to let my feelings flow.

Writing out the word is easier,
as the ink flows and flows,
but the other me wants to be heard,
not just read and put away, like a forgotten rose.

So bear with me, I'll find my voice,
with every trial and every choice,
I'll learn to speak with confidence and grace,
and move forward to a better place.

DRESS IN BLUE

On the green meadow side,
She stood in her plain cotton dress in blue,
As the wind blew, her dress danced along with it
Like a clear stream flowing, during mid summer
Dressed in blue, a piece of the sky she seemed to be
That landed on for venturing forth to seek and see
As her eyes scanned over the distant horizon.

Beautifully wrapped around,
Her curves like lush mountains,
A scenery of blue - green
A replica of God's hand in nature.
The bronze glow in her hair,
Radiates even more,
As the sunrays gleam over her.

The sky is clearer than ever,
The grassy meadows swayed along with the wind,
A gesture of their delight.
And the wildflower welcomed her by blooming brighter,
A beauty so pure, no mistake,
A revival of springtime.

FLAME

If you have ever stopped,
Painting your dreams,
And if your dreams are smeared like colours,
But the picture never seemed to be an absolute.

When you have visualized,
How bright it would be,
But all you ever paint is in Grey's.

A ball of fire within,
Yet a drop of tear would douse it.
Alas! It would now take an eternity,
To burn that flame again.

GAS LIGHTING

Some words take us downhill,
A loop of constant confusion and uncertainty
Of what ifs and whys
How twisted can they be,
To drag you out of your reality.
Only to end up making you question your sanity,
With every comment and critique,
We feel a hole in our very soul,
The state of mind, always in a conflict,
And its hard to say which is real.
Perhaps the answer lies within,
Alas! The confusion now rooted deep within,
And the clarity that we seek
Seem to be a distant vision.
Can we ever question their absurdity?
Or to accept their distorted reality,
Tagged as paranoid, if we ever stand up,
Against their deceit.
A subtle art to tear the mind apart,
A way to doubt the perception,
To make a clouded judgement,
To keep us stuck in a hole, to never see the truth.

A game of twist-and-turn,
Stage one- your confidence starts to burn,
And here we are again, down to shambles,
Wondering what we had, was ever a grounded reality.
Oh so sly with words, a seamless web,
Of manipulation designed,
To keep us stuck in our place,
And prevent from seeking liberation.

JUMBLED

Words collide with my mind,
Confusion, now a safe haven no more.
How miserable can one be
To accept this state of being?

One path after another,
And it leads to none.
A never-ending journey,
With no destination.

Life once felt like a path of knots,
Never an easy slide.
Stumbling along the way,
This mind has been stuck for way too long.

But now I see a glimmer of hope,
A chance to find my missing puzzle piece.
Years went by and I was numb,
A puzzle waiting to be solved,
A scrambled mess of thoughts and fear,
The jumbled mess that brings tears.

Yet, with each day, my mind grows clearer,
Scrambled letters and words now form a story.
I search for focus, clarity,
And find my way out of the maze of vanity.

Jumbled thoughts become clear as day
Words starts to make their way
Missing piece starts to fit

The stories I write now,
Reflect the reality that I live in.
No longer a jumbled mess,
But a beautiful symphony of words.

VISION

Envision yourself as a butterfly ,
When you feel stuck in a cocoon.
Your dreams are too radiant,
It wants to be among the Stars.

CLARITY

Life, a misty haze
Like a dewy morning in the fall
A blissful uncertainty lingers,
Like a dream that we can't recall.
A phase of everything;
That is unclear and nostalgic
A stage in life where clarity
Is a fight that must be won
A gift of being an adult.
With faith, we float above obstacles
With, strength we forge ahead.

www.ingramcontent.com/pod-product-compliance
Lightning Source LLC
LaVergne TN
LVHW061600070526
838199LV00077B/7127